LITTLE LIBRARY

First 200 Words in
Spanish

Candi Perez & Juan Luis Montoussé
Illustrated by Katy Sleight

Kingfisher Books

NEW YORK

Contents

All about your book	5
Your body	6
Things to wear	8
Playtime	10
At home	12
Animals	14
On the move	16
At the beach	18
Things to do	20
Opposites	22
Months and seasons	24
Counting and colors	26
Word square	28
Word list	29

All about your book

Your Little Library picture dictionary will help you learn your first 200 words in Spanish.

The Spanish words are printed in heavy type (**el gato**) and appear with the English word beside a picture of the word. You will see that most of the Spanish words have a small word before them, meaning "the" (**el, la, los,** or **las**). When you learn these words, don't forget to learn the word for "the," too.

If you hear people speaking Spanish, you will notice that many of the sounds they use are quite different from the ones we use in English. So ask a parent or teacher, or best of all a Spanish-speaking person, how to say the words correctly.

You can test some of the words you have learned by doing the word square puzzle at the end of the dictionary.

Your body

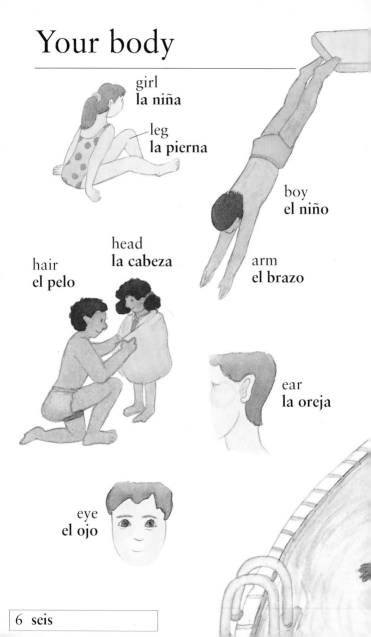

girl
la niña

leg
la pierna

boy
el niño

head
la cabeza

hair
el pelo

arm
el brazo

ear
la oreja

eye
el ojo

nose
la nariz

finger
el dedo

teeth
los dientes

mouth
la boca

tongue
la lengua

hand
la mano

foot
el pie

Things to wear

T-shirt
la camiseta

jeans
los pantalones tejanos

shoes
los zapatos

dress
el vestido

raincoat
el impermeable/ la gabardina

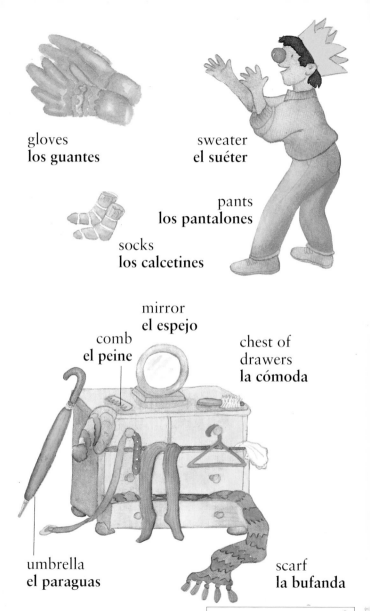

gloves
los guantes

sweater
el suéter

pants
los pantalones

socks
los calcetines

mirror
el espejo

comb
el peine

chest of
drawers
la cómoda

umbrella
el paraguas

scarf
la bufanda

Playtime

book
el libro

train set
el tren de juguete

teddy bear
el oso de peluche

spinning top
el trompo

slide
**el tobogán/
la resbaladilla**

roller skates
los patines

jump rope
**la cuerda/
la comba**

puppet
**el títere/
la marioneta**

paints
las pinturas

pencils
los lápices

At home

bathroom
el cuarto de baño   toilet
el lavabo

kitchen
la cocina

door
la puerta

sink
el fregadero

chair
la silla

window
la ventana

clock
el reloj

curtain
la cortina

bedroom
el dormitorio

house
la casa

bed
la cama

floor
el suelo

radio
la radio

television
**la televisión/
el televisor**

painting
el cuadro

wall
a pared

table
la mesa

sofa
el sofá

iving room
a sala

bookcase
el estante

Animals

butterfly
la mariposa

bird
el pájaro

spider
la araña

dog
el perro

bee
la abeja

tiger
el tigre

elephant
el elefante

fish
el pez

wolf
el lobo

mouse
el ratón

horse
el caballo

cat
el gato

monkey
el mono

sheep
la oveja

lion
el león

lioness
la leona

On the move

airplane
el avión

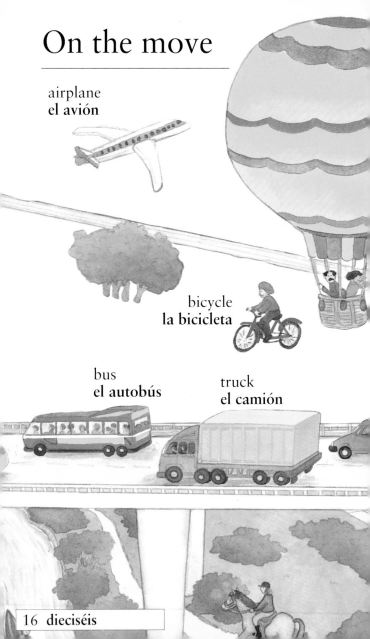

bicycle
la bicicleta

bus
el autobús

truck
el camión

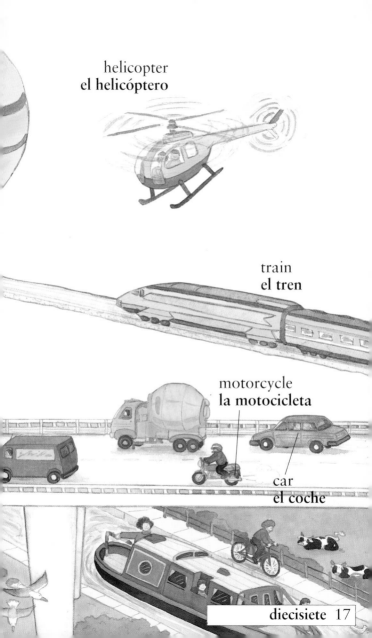

helicopter
el helicóptero

train
el tren

motorcycle
la motocicleta

car
el coche

At the beach

ship
el barco

motorboat
la lancha

wave
la ola

shovel
la pala

pail
el cubo/la cubeta

shell
la concha

sea
el mar

lighthouse
el faro

rock
la roca

sand castle
**el castillo
de arena**

seaweed
el alga

sand
la arena

beach
la playa

ice cream
el helado

Things to do

open
abrir

write
escribir

read
leer

father
el padre

hold
sostener

pull
tirar

cry
llorar

carry
llevar

run
correr

listen
escuchar

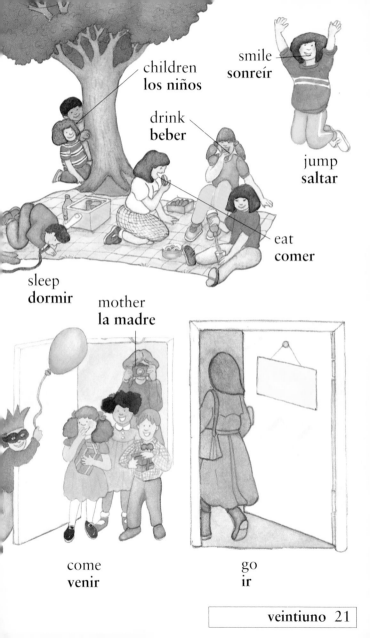

smile
sonreír

children
los niños

drink
beber

jump
saltar

eat
comer

sleep
dormir

mother
la madre

come
venir

go
ir

Opposites

full
lleno

empty
vacío

on the left
a la izquierda

on the right
a la derecha

warm
caliente

in front of
delante de

cold
frío

behind
detrás

long
largo

dry
seco

wet
mojado

short
corto

old
viejo

new
nuevo

big
grande

open
abierto

shut
cerrado

little
pequeño

clean
limpio

dirty
sucio

slow
lento

fast
rápido

easy
fácil

difficult
difícil

2+2 = 7⟌22369

Months and seasons

January
enero

February
febrero

March
marzo

April
abril

May
mayo

June
junio

spring
la primavera

sun
el sol

summer
el verano

July
julio

August
agosto

September
septiembre

October
octubre

November
noviembre

December
diciembre

fall
el otoño

rain
la lluvia

winter
el invierno

snow
la nieve

Counting and colors

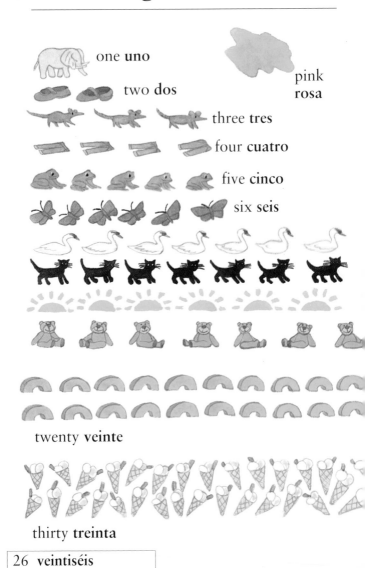

one **uno**

pink **rosa**

two **dos**

three **tres**

four **cuatro**

five **cinco**

six **seis**

twenty **veinte**

thirty **treinta**

blue
azul

black
negro

brown
marrón/café

purple
morado

green
verde

yellow
amarillo

red
rojo

seven **siete**

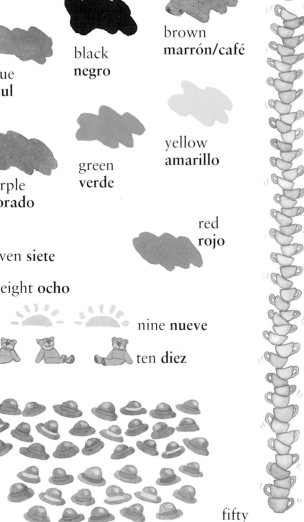

eight **ocho**

nine **nueve**

ten **diez**

forty **cuarenta**

fifty
cincuenta

Word square

Can you find the six Spanish words hidden in this square? The pictures will help you guess the words.

m	s	p	e	r	r	o
t	i	p	j	k	h	a
r	l	n	b	t	e	w
f	l	e	e	r	l	m
c	a	b	e	z	a	v
o	i	t	g	s	d	d
k	q	r	o	j	o	x

Word list

airplane el avión
April abril
arm el brazo
August agosto

bathroom el cuarto de baño
beach la playa
bed la cama
bedroom el dormitorio
bee la abeja
behind detrás
bicycle la bicicleta
big grande
bird el pájaro
black negro
blue azul
book el libro
bookcase el estante
boy el niño
brown marrón/café
bus el autobús
butterfly la mariposa

car el coche
carry llevar
cat el gato
chair la silla
chest of drawers la cómoda
children los niños
clean limpio
clock el reloj
cold frío
comb el peine
come venir
cry llorar
curtain la cortina

December diciembre
difficult difícil
dirty sucio
dog el perro
door la puerta
dress el vestido
drink beber
dry seco

ear la oreja
easy fácil

eat comer
eight ocho
elephant el elefante
empty vacío
eye el ojo

fall el otoño
fast rápido
father el padre
February febrero
fifty cincuenta
finger el dedo
fish el pez
five cinco
floor el suelo
foot el pie
forty cuarenta
four cuatro
full lleno

girl la niña
gloves los guantes
go ir
green verde

hair el pelo
hand la mano
head la cabeza
helicopter el helicóptero
hold sostener
horse el caballo
house la casa

ice cream el helado
in front of delante de

January enero
jeans los pantalones tejanos
July julio
jump saltar
jump rope la cuerda/la comba
June junio

kitchen la cocina

(on the) left a la izquierda
leg la pierna
lighthouse el faro
lion el león
lioness la leona

listen escuchar
little pequeño
living room la sala
long largo

March marzo
May mayo
mirror el espejo
monkey el mono
mother la madre
motorcycle la motocicleta
motorboat la lancha
mouse el ratón
mouth la boca

new nuevo
nine nueve
nose la nariz
November noviembre

October octubre
old viejo
one uno
open abierto
(to) open abrir

pail un cubo
painting el cuadro
paints las pinturas
pants los pantalones
pencils los lápices
pink rosa
pull tirar
puppet el títere/la marioneta
purple morado

radio la radio
rain la lluvia
raincoat el impermeable
read leer
red rojo
(on the) right a la derecha
rock la roca
roller skates los patines
run correr
sand la arena
sand castle el castillo de arena
scarf la bufanda
sea el mar
seaweed el alga
September septiembre
seven siete

sheep la oveja
shell la concha
ship el barco
shoes los zapatos
short corto
shovel la pala
shut cerrado
sink el fregadero
six seis
sleep dormir
slide el tobogán/la resbaladilla
slow lento
smile sonreír
snow la nieve
socks los calcetines
sofa el sofá
spider la araña
spinning top el trompo
spring la primavera
summer el verano
sun el sol
sweater el suéter

table la mesa
teddy bear el oso de peluche
teeth los dientes
television el televisor/la televisión
ten diez
thirty treinta
three tres
tiger el tigre
toilet el lavabo
tongue la lengua
train el tren
train set el tren de juguete
truck el camión
T-shirt la camiseta
twenty veinte
two dos

umbrella el paraguas

wall la pared
warm caliente
wave la ola
wet mojado
window la ventana
winter el invierno
wolf el lobo
write escribir

yellow amarillo